salmonpoetry

Publishing Irish & International

Poetry Since 1981

at the last minute
estha weiner

Published in 2019 by
Salmon Poetry
Cliffs of Moher, County Clare, Ireland
Website: www.salmonpoetry.com
Email: info@salmonpoetry.com

ISBN 978-1-912561-53-7

Cover & Title Page Photography: *Michael Ian.* Post-production: *Eileen Travell*
Cover Design & Typesetting: *Siobhán Hutson*

Printed in Ireland by Sprint Print

*Salmon Poetry gratefully acknowledges the support of
The Arts Council / An Chomhairle Ealaíon*

"Enormous Changes At The Last Minute"...

GRACE PALEY

For Jimmy,

"The wind does not forget but carries what it can."

J. TOLAN

For Dal,

If only Macky were back in town…

and

For Bernie Jazz

Acknowledgements

Thank you to the editors of the following publications/books in which these poems appeared:

JJournal – "Two Days After" (Nominated for a Pushcart Prize)

Hurricane Blues (anthology), S.E. Missouri State University Press – "New Orleans Has Collapsed"

JJournal - "Lying About Sex"

Even the Daybreak: 35 Years of Salmon Poetry - " ...to the sea again" (Salmon Poetry, 2016)

Westchester Review – "Cleavage"

Some poems have appeared in *In the Weather of the World* (Salmon Poetry, 2013).

Like Light: 25 Years of Poetry and Prose by Bright Hill Poets and Writers (anthology). Bright Hill Press—"Paul and Joanne" and "Who do you think you are,"

Contents

"Don't ever grow old, Bill," 13

Two Days After: 14

New Orleans Has Collapsed 15

Kafka, Intimately 16

And there's still free Shakespeare in The Park 17

Exit, pursued by bear 18

Cleavage 19

For All The Girls Who Love Them 20

Hands, 21

The Meeting 22

At Home 23

Captive Audience 24

Paul and Joanne 25

Who do you think you are, 26

Match 27

"What is so rare as a day in June…?" 28

Lying About Sex 29

This Poetry's Reading's * 'Suffered a Diminuendo
in Personnel'… 31

Immune 32

The Club 33

4:30 in the Morning 34

Hole I Day 35

Old Lines/New Lines 36

Bright Girl Wanted 37

This country's 38

Two Turkeys Are Being Pardoned 39

'Please hold while we retrieve history,'   40

Fifty years ago   41

From the A to Z List   42

More and More Myrrh   43

Swerves   44

In the pool of the jury there are many vowels   46

Put The Blame on Maine   47

The Vermonter   48

Notions   50

The Creed of the Baron   51

Performance Art   52

Savage Beauty   53

Acquired Tastes   54

Stage Directions For Father's Day   55

Fedora   56

When a Formal Feeling Comes   57

Mothballs Are For Mothers   58

Superior Florists   59

Be Care Ful   60

Dialogue   61

Found: Wilde Cinquains   62

Protest   63

At 5:45 pm in the Conservatory Garden   64

This is what happens   65

…to the sea again   66

About the author   69

"Don't ever grow old, Bill,"

for W. M.

his 99-year-old grandmother
commanded as she approached
the nearly mythic,
and he, contrary
to the end,
chose this one,
only this one
to obey.

Two Days After:

Finally, some sun.
From my fire escape
terrace—I look out
on another roof—
astro-turfed, lounge-chaired,
picnic-tabled, planted—
see the sculptor
spray painting his
two rectangular shapes
black.

Then, on the phone
from her farm
on the west coast
of England, Carol tells me
her daughter was all dressed
for her first Disco Night
at school, wearing the glitter
tee shirt she'd wanted, when
Carol realized
the New York skyline, the two towers
on her daughter's tiny breasts.

New Orleans Has Collapsed!

In Appreciation of Frank O'Hara

I was watching the hurricane news,
thinking it's bad but it's not as bad
as they thought when all of a sudden
it was worse   why??   the levees broke
and the water poured through the sexy sweet
City of New Orleans through
cemeteries and jazz
Zydeco and oysters
booze and Blues
balconies and Brennan's
Black and White

Congregation Named Desire
Queen of the River Excess
did the God of those Righteous Boys
now running
the U.S. of A.
visit this flood upon your sensuous
banks No Noah in these Boys' plans
Oh New Orleans   I love you   get up!

Kafka, Intimately

She knew it,
(daughter of Survivors),
knew one morning
you could wake, transformed
into vermin,
no matter
your gifts,
your beauty, no
matter even that lucky love
surrounding you,
wake to the moment
when the world
would desecrate your prayer
for even a semblance
of sanity.

And there's still free Shakespeare in The Park

The stage rotates, complete
with moat and arc of bridge
for Montagues and Capulets.
This Juliet's red tresses glow
as the sun sets on order
of both directors.
Sound carries in the night.
Suddenly, not from the stage:
"Sieg Heil! Heil Hitler!" stabs
our Shakespeare, sprung from a script
unspeakable, a prank
of punks. We hope,
and reel attention back
to Juliet, who might wake
in time, this time.

Exit, pursued by bear

When I was paid
to wear a mask,

I lauded authenticity,
off-stage, as well as on,

transparency, the open
book, the open vein: my song.

All the world is still
a stage, though I'm a different player.

It seems the mask works just as well
off-stage as it works on,

taming that unruly shrew
we nick-name honesty.

Cleavage

English is a little devil. One or
more principles could also be
missing from love, and if you
didn't read carefully, you wouldn't
know you might be cleaving to your
beloved, even as your beloved was
cleaving your heart in twain, even as
he or she was daily raising your hopes,
he or she, simultaneously, was razing
the foundations on which those hopes
were resting, even as he or she was
wresting the tender, as if that were
the principal meaning of be loved.

"For so much of love,
one of the principals
is missing"
— WILLIAM MATTHEWS

For All The Girls Who Love Them

"Are you a pirate?"
asked the little girl.
"Then where's the treasure?"

They kidnap
with or without eye patch,
even though girls know better,
because knowing, at its worst's
not knowing, so
they take you, make you
walk the plank of their Captain,
the tightrope of their circus,
the dread of their desire,
the delight of their danger,
and it becomes all
there is to know,
and you are hooked,
while the alligator lies
in wait, for the chance
to eat one of your hands.

Hands,

like a Hungarian worker,
he called his own—Later
I would compare them
to the other's long, slender,
patrician artist fingers,
the blues of the world
slipping through, as I
was left
to do,
through these, as through
the stocky solid pair,
with almost equal
ease and death-
defying skill.

The Meeting

First, the blood anticipates,
speeding to the actual
appearance, to the clasp
of bodies, then
a hand reaches up
to touch the memorized
face, to trace
the outline of the lips
finally there, waiting for
the kiss, to verify.

At Home

I like to be alone with love,
sit silent,
protect it

from someone else's harm,
intentional or un-.

Safe and saved,
it stays in the day,
does not stray in the night,

dines well with me
by candlelight.

Captive Audience

"Talk To Me Like The Rain And Let Me Listen"

—TENNESSEE WILLIAMS

1.
In the play, it's The Man
who asks her
to talk to him. Yes
is all The Woman says.
No one worries
about role reversal:
It's a play.

2.
The Woman does not say
Talk to me.
You never talk to me.
The Man says he will lie
there and listen
if The Woman will
just talk to him.

3.
I will always lie
there and listen
when The Man uses words
righter even than rain.
If he lies,
I will love
each perfect word.

Paul and Joanne

"Last of the great broads,"
he called her, and when he left
the world, he'd been with the broad
for fifty years, from The Long Hot Summer,
From the Terrace, Rachel, Rachel,
Mr. and Mrs. Bridge: Winning.
It may not all have been a Picnic,
but theirs was a story to love.

Necessary for love is memory.
Seven years later,
she's now lost most
of both, but still remembers this:
"I used to be married to someone very handsome."

Who do you think you are,

Sarah Bernhardt? Jewish
parents, apparently in addition
to mine, loved to pop as a question,
which, being Jewish, was really
an answer, disguised as a question:
"You, with the drama,
enough already!" My mother
acted, on stage and off;
my father acted like he wished
he were in the audience. I became
an actor, and missed his last
hours upon the stage
that all the world is,
because I had a second audition
for a show,
which must go on.

Match

You gotta train
for this kind of love:
stay in shape,
top of your game,
ready for the quick
jab, the second
kiss   good   bye.
Only short rests against
the rope,
eyes open,
dance of offence,
defense indefensible.
Be sensible.
Don't ask.

"What is so rare as a day in June...?"

Afterwards, I only wanted
to buy flowers, more
and more flowers,
as if their petals
would protect if they fell
on the unprotected,
as if they would,
as if they could.

Lying About Sex

"Elizabeth, I have confessed"

—John Proctor, *The Crucible,* Arthur Miller

I thought I saw
my husband

What of Abigail Williams?

somewhat turning from

Goody Proctor

My husband is a good
and righteous

To your own knowledge,
has John Proctor

I came to think
he fancied

Your husband—
did he

My husband
is a goodly

Then he
did not

He is a goodly

Has John Proctor ever
committed the crime

He

Is your husband
a lecher?

No, sir.

This Poetry Reading's* 'Suffered a Diminuendo in Personnel'

The third poet
from the left
reads with his glasses
pushed to the bridge
of his nose, in that pose
or non-pose
you used to adopt
then had to mock
because nothing could be more
than the light
touch of the self-
conscious yet elegant,
who finally
is not above
giving or receiving
the attack
of the heart.

* from "Mingus at the Showplace" by William Matthews

Immune

"Death is the mother of beauty"—

WALLACE STEVENS

If you are tall, lean,
close to heart-harrowing handsome,
working on well-known,
or full-blown famous,
ride a bicycle or a horse,
eat holy grains
or harvested salmon,
no cells of yours
can be invaded,
no blood or bone
impenetrated;
no paralysis dare seize
your muscles
'til even a swallow
of water's impossible.

If you are tall, lean
and close
to heart-harrowing
handsome, none of this
can ever happen.

The Club

The way a baby always
notices another baby—
That's the way I noticed
every other cripple,
permanent or temporary, after
my leg was wrapped in bandages,
so only I could see the gash.

Or the way they noticed me,
stared at one wrapped leg
and one tanned leg, both defiant,
sticking out there
under my short skirt. The woman
with metal crutches, the man
who could barely fit
his wheelchair on the bus,
and the driver who had to wait.

4:30 in the Morning

The dogs of Pavlov wake me every day,
same time, consistent, do not rest, so why
should I? Each terror, worry, plague they lay
before my sleeping feet, then start to pry

the chance for any peace or any more;
from toes to calves to knees and then to thighs,
begin to toss and turn me till the chore
of closing back my eyes takes twenty tries.

Then I give up, give in to ceiling stares.
Obsession and compulsion steal the quilts,
or just the dogs of Pavlov on a tear:
They snarl each fear, each loss, and every guilt.

Until I check the clock for affirmation:
It's just that time of day, and it'll pass—
        Be patient.

Hole I Day

Yes, here's another one:
Like the groundhog, it comes out
full-tilt boogie or casts a fat shadow,
taunting me, a true believer, to keep
the faith, flimsy as it be; to conjure
the magic, which the occasional one
has produced, to recall the spark
of a day set apart, despite the flat
flavor of the one immediately
before me, to affirm the necessity
of ceremony, of even the tentative
expectations of perfection.

Old Lines

No fear then: Hit the Road and Hitch
to Stratford for The Dream, Peter Brook's and ours,
got us through the night, to the ticket queue
already there at 6 am, orderly English
offerings of Tea? Milk? as we hoped for Oberon and Puck
to sparkle Midsummer upon our hunger for wonder.

New Lines

Two years anticipation, two hours in line
for the perfect Lobster Roll, at Red's Eats,
Wiscasset, prettiest little village in Maine,
Red's: fresh off front page of Times Travel
Section: larger than usual tidal wave at Red's.
45 minutes in, nice girl comes out with dog biscuit
for hungry dog in front of me: 60 minutes in, another girl
hands out free fried shrimp, one per human; 70 minutes in,
original nice person brings out bowl of water
for thirsty (formerly hungry dog) in front
of me. It's my turn. Another nice girl behind
counter gives me large order of fries, even
though I'd only paid for small, offers
me mayonnaise AND butter instead of mayonnaise
OR butter for the perfect Lobster Roll that is
finally mine.

Bright Girl Wanted

for Lois

That he could stand up there, alone,
the quiet one of the pair, (she was
said to provide the flair), both,
with the long grey hair (his tied
neatly at the neck, as a doctor
would, who has long grey hair),

That he could stand up there, alone:
"Let me tell you about my wife."
(Let me tell you about my friend, his wife:
A tooth abscess spread to her brain.)
(That I sit here and write this.)
"Our beautiful, brilliant Mother."
That her children could stand up there, alone.
"Let me tell you about my wife:
She got her first job from *The N. Y. Times*,
an Ad. you couldn't write today:

(He met her in college.)
(She went on to Columbia.)
(He went to medical school.)
(They were married for 40 years.)

"an Ad. you could not write today:
'BRIGHT GIRL WANTED.'"

This country's

bleak and green,
as if allowing too much
sun in one day
would be indulgence.
Better to parcel out in patches,
abruptly shift to wind
and then the rain,
to keep us rather
off balance,
though we learn to be
prepared, to comment
on the quixotic,
and keep as dry as possible.

Two Turkeys Are Being Pardoned for Thanksgiving and Staying in a Washington Hotel That Costs Between $300-$3,000 a Night

One of the turkey's sisters
may not be so lucky

One of the turkey's brothers
may get the same room
same time next year

Both turkeys' parents
are dead

One man without a home sneaks
in between the two turkeys
and makes it
to their door

One man without a green card
borrows one of the turkey's
key cards

Both of the turkeys are still
hungry: Not enough food
in their hotel room

Neither of the turkeys know
how to call Room Service

They may starve
to death in their hotel room

"Please hold while we retrieve history."

(as if it were nothing
to retrieve, much less
to hold)
requests the cheerful
voice of Amalgamated Bank,
custodian of deposits and withdrawals,
of credits and debits.
Teletronic fairy godmother,
grant my chronic
hindsight-haunted wishes, go
retrieve history.
I promise this
time I will hold.

Fifty years ago,

they gave her a bouquet
of roses   (remember?),
darker than the pink
of the famous stunning
suit, closer
to the color of the blood
on the famous
stunning suit (Chanel,
wasn't it?)

"She's breakin' my ass,"
he was said to have complained
about the money
she used to spend, sounding
like the Irish
tough-assed enchanter I myself
had loved, and how
could I not,
how could she not,
how could we not
have loved?

From the A to Z List

Access to lilacs
Bones of alone
Collapse of cushion
Death of dreary
Excess of excellent
Fill of ill
Gasp of asp
Hit of wit
I of I
Jolt of jeopardy
Kick that trick
Love
Midway in my...
No theatre
On to gone
Possible possible
Queue of cues
Roll the rock
Stock up
Transfiguration begins
Under the sun
Vignette of cigarette
Whisp of wisdom
X-ray of ex-
Y?
Zip

More and More Myrrh

If its gifts
can glide
between the Three Magi
and Solomon's
groom and bride,

If the gummy dried sap
offers itself
to the mix of medicine,
incense, perfume,
and embalming,

If under a Somali
baby's bed
it is placed
with hope
to shape the future,

If it comes
from the word
"maror" : bitter
herb eaten
for ritual reminder,

If the same Wise Man
(magician?) who brought it
to a manger
brought it to a Crucifixion
to anoint,

then it must
know   more
than we ever will.

"A bundle of myrrh is
my well-beloved unto me."
    from THE SONG OF SOLOMON

Swerves

1.

"I wanna be a part of it..."

On the #1 train, an older man plays his horn
and a recorded music box, while holding a cup
for contributions. Down the aisle, from the other
end, comes a young man with no legs, propelling
his chair. "How ya doin,' Alex?" asks the older
man with a horn. "Hey, it's New York," answers
the young man with no legs. The older man nods
and plays "If I can make it there, I'll make it
anywhere."

2.

"...who made oranges grow in the desert"

Because the last Orthodox rabbi was murdered,
Ruth's son now has a job as a bodyguard for
the new Orthodox rabbi, who is still in danger
because one of his tasks is to bless The Palestinian
Pickle Factory, to make sure the Palestinian pickles
are Kosher.

3.

Be Nine

Is Kim Jung ill?
Asp me no questions:
We were between Iraq
and a hard place.
(Ode on aggression earned)
Sin agog:
It's Yahweh or The Highway.

4.

Whiplash

From accolade
to penny count, penny
count to accolade,
count to account:
No account
in the penny arcade.

In the pool of the jury there are many vowels

Barack Obama
Wins Iowa

Ithaca's called Odysseus
home to Penelope
for three thousand years

"A, I, E" make Maine's
accent haven for lobstahs
and home for Estha

Venom drips
through my neighbors' Virginia
vowels, as they pronounce
the word "Jews."

Daily we
discover America

Put The Blame On Maine

1.

After Bette left him,
(After ALL ABOUT EVE),
Gary stayed in our home
town, drinking more and more,
strolling the length of the piers,
rarely stopping to buy a lobster.

2.

Before she left him, Bette Davis
directed our Christmas Pageant,
commanding miniature lords and ladies
to sword and garland dance
with zest, to carry
a paper-mache boar's head, while singing
"The Boar's Head Carol," then exit
with "Joy to the World."

3.

When Gary's heart began
to heal, he drank
a little less, was seen
around town a little more,
each event a rehearsal for that
starry starry day
Gary Merrill took Rita Hayworth
to the Bowdoin-Williams game.

The Vermonter

Waxing poetic about trains, as usual,
is   just   what I was doing
when The Vermonter pulled out of hot Gotham,
for the Green Mountains,
in the only state safe for socialism.

Two young dancers, one White, one Black
stretch then move down the aisle.
The conductor calls:
"Hello, ballerinas!
Where do you go to school?"

He stops to ask two little boys
if they've got their licenses with them.
(They just told him they wanted
to drive the train.)

One stunning young actor
meets another stunning young actor
who's going to work
at the same summer theatre.

There's a one-hour delay in Springfield.
There's no more air-conditioning

except in one car, where I run.
Another conductor is discussing *The Scarlet Letter*
with a passenger with a Puritan past
and a new degree in American Lit.

Then the conductor speaks French
to an affectionate couple
on their way to Montreal.

Another delay at the Vermont border:
A tree's fallen across the tracks.
We wait for the man
with the chain-saw.

As the sun starts to set,
we pull into White River Junction:
"Hey," says The Conductor, "just two hours late."

Notions

Many years I have marveled
at the survival
of The Chelsea Sewing Center,
whose awning boasted: "Notions,
Fabrics, Buttons," to whom I
turned for all of the above,
but most particularly, buttons,
for which I might call ahead
to see not only if she had
the necessary one, but more
often than not, to see
if the store were open,
which depended on its owner, only,
beautiful, brazen, knowledgeable,
her improbable existence
vital to a New York gone
mad with real estate and fake unique,
vital, 'til today, when my worst
fears faced me: only awning remaining
over vacant window,
except for hand-written sign:
"Cartridge World Coming Soon."

The Creed of the Baron

You gotta break a strike,
get out the crude,
railroad the country,
steal the steel
if you wanna
make a museum,
carve out a park,
preserve a forest,
build a library:
Read your Bible,
Read your Bible:
Better to give
than to receive.

Performance Art

You don't see this every day:
Two Nudes on Floor, on
Canvas, never more, at MOMA:

Two Nudes on Floor, face
Each other in between
Two exhibition spaces

Two models paid to stand
Nude on MOMA's floor
From opening to close

We nearly touch them
As we pass from one
Room to another

One girl, one woman
Stand nude and stare
Into each other's eyes

Nearby, the guard stands also
As he's paid to do:
He does not stare at the two.

He stands on MOMA's floor
From opening to close
With all his clothes on

He'll still be there
When the ladies aren't
Standing on MOMA's floor.

Savage Beauty

*"'Alexander McQueen:
Savage Beauty' has shattered
the Metropolitan Museum's
attendance record...
He committed suicide at
the age of 40."*

AM NEW YORK

That New Yorkers who give standing
ovations at the drop of any curtain
would think nothing of standing in line
for hours, fanning themselves
near the Florence and Herbert Irving
Asian Wing

(And he'd even dressed
the new Princess)

If he'd known,
would he still
abjure the rough magic?

("This thing of darkness
I acknowledge mine!")

He knew the stuff
that dreams are made on:

If you want it
You gotta wait
in line.

"I want people to be afraid
of the women I dress."

"I especially like the acces-
ory for its masochistic
aspect."

"The Victorian Era greatly
influenced me: the austerity,
the severity, the melancholy."

"What Britain did there is
nothing short of genocide."

"It started off dark and got
more romantic as it went
along."

"There's no way back for me
now. I'm going to take you
on journeys you never
dreamed were possible."

Acquired Tastes

One red ankle-strap shoe
fell through the Barnum
and Bailey bleachers
when we came to the big city.

One shoe off and one shoe on,
locked in the Mummy Room
at The Museum of Natural History.

That painting of Eloise,
my heroine, at The Plaza Hotel?
They hung it on the wall for me.

Then they taught me to eat an oyster,
and to play stud and draw
poker, with blue chips.

Stage Directions For Father's Day

Paint toes red.
Pretend you were there to soften the dread.
Polish the wit
When the images hit.

Fedora

The hat business,
he used to say,
died the day
J.F.K. walked bare-
headed down Pennsylvania
Avenue, in honor of
youth, thick hair, and vigah.

With thick, greyer hair
than the new President,
he'd worn the hat through the Great Depression
and through his wife's, through
The War, the opening
of MY FAIR LADY, The Four Seasons,
and the birth of his dark
little girl.

In her 26th year, she
lost him. She took
the brown felt, hand-
blocked by Cavanagh's,
his initials woven in gold thread
on the inside rim,   took it
out to wear, always
returning it
to the box, with care.

In her 50th year,
(his age at the birth of this dark little girl),
she lost it.
She searched madly, constantly,
madly, quietly.

When a Formal Feeling Comes

"After great pain,
a formal feeling
comes"

   —Dickinson

Chew what you can't taste,
ten times more than necessary.
There is actually a lump in your throat.
Keep talking
'til sound finds sense.
Walk with effort,
feet, bound.
Back and forth.
Back and forth.
Choose the highest necked,
longest sleeved garment
to cover everything,
particularly your chest
cavity.   Then
the knob on the door. You
can leave.

Mothballs Are For Mothers

Without those little globes, you lose
two coats, two sweaters, one
black cape (all drama):

holes so huge
as to be unpatchable, eaten away
by creatures focused on one thing

while you were busy
not repairing worn-down heels,
ignoring investment strategy, signs

of waning interest,
and the day after tomorrow,
when he wouldn't be able
to fix it anymore.

Superior Florists

On more than difficult days,
she buys two calla lilies,
preferably purple, though she accepts
pure white, if the purple have been sold.

She jokes with the shopowner
in a Katherine Hepburn voice; he gives
her a discount and extra leaves,
and she thinks of her mother:

How few things other than flowers made her mother
happy. How her mother would buy calla lillies
and cry   Where is my daughter?

She is here. She is
here. She is here, and you
will not find her.

Be   Care   Ful

Just one or two
plants to fill
the empty window

boxes, once lavish
in festooned flora,
now recession lean,

though residues
of lavish live
in the perennials

(Once
upon a time
there was a gardener)

and a well-taken-care-of
young lady, tenderer
today, of possible blossoms.

Dialogue

Come, dearest, we'll play
A little poker,
Stud and Draw,
The first game you taught me.
I'll bring our plastic chips;
You'll win. I'll take
Your hand. I'll take
You out of here.
Listen, I'm pretending
I can talk to you.
Pretend you can
Hear me.
Come, dearest,
Come back.

Found: Wilde Cinquains

"To lose
one parent may
be regarded as a
misfortune. To lose both looks like
carelessness."

"The thing
about dust is
that after the first sev-
en years, no one notices."   Os-
car Wilde

Protest

At midnight, contrary
to girls in fairy tales, I want
not to watch golden coaches turn
back into pumpkins, or to watch
myself or Cinderella or anyone
be reduced to sweeping dust
again. I want no more
midnights, if
that's what their strokes bring
to anyone or anything
changing shape, with the luck
of a wand or not.
Let the white mice
prance us out.

At 5:45 pm in The Conservatory Garden

The crow comes to drink
from Pan's fountain,
which spills
into the lily pond
as the light sweetens
the day's inevitable slide
into evening, into late
August. That dark bird, out
of place amongst   the   lavenders
and roses, takes
off, with me
tempted to follow.

This is what happens

Sometimes I have to sit down,
I miss you so much.

Have to pull up a chair,
my socks, dust off

my shoes,   stand again
on my size 9 feet,

place one foot before
the other,

start to move
forwards, keep

going, keep
going until

I find another
place to sit down,

I miss you
so much.

... to the sea again

In the waves
the voices of the lost
are found

In the gentle lap
or the undertow
the whitecaps whisper
the beloved they know

Or the whitecaps spit
their relentless snare

Either way they drown
us. It's why we're there

ESTHA WEINER's newest poetry collection is *at the last minute* (Salmon Poetry, 2019). She is author of *In the Weather of the World* (Salmon Poetry); *The Mistress Manuscript* (Asheville Book Works); *Transfiguration Begins At Home* (Tiger Bark Press); and co-editor/contributor to *Blues for Bill: A Tribute to William Matthews* (Akron Poetry Series, University of Akron Press).   Her poems have appeared in numerous anthologies and magazines, including *The New Republic* and *Barrow Street*, and six poems have been translated into Dutch. Winner of a Paterson Poetry Prize and a Visiting Scholar at The Shakespeare Institute, Stratford, England, Estha is founding director of Sarah Lawrence College NY Alumni/ae Writers Nights, Marymount Writers Nights, and a Speaker on Shakespeare for New York Council For The Humanities. She is a Professor at City University of NY, and Sarah Lawrence College Writing Institute and serves or has served on the Poetry/Writing faculties of The Frost Place, Hudson Valley Writers Center, Stone Coast Writers Conference, Poets and Writers, Poets House, and The Writers Voice. She also serves on the Advisory Committee of Slapering Hol Press, Hudson Valley Writers Center. In her previous life, Estha was an actor and worked for BBC Radio.

salmonpoetry
Cliffs of Moher, County Clare, Ireland

*"Like the sea-run Steelhead salmon that thrashes upstream to its spawning
ground, then instead of dying, returns to the sea – Salmon Poetry Press
brings precious cargo to both Ireland and America in the poetry it publishes,
then carries that select work to its readership against incalculable odds."*

TESS GALLAGHER

The Salmon Bookshop
& Literary Centre

Ennistymon, County Clare, Ireland

"Another wonderful Clare outlet."
The Irish Times, 35 Best Independent Bookshops